START-UP
RELIGION

VISITING A MOSQUE

Ruth Nason

CHERRYTREE BOOKS

Distributed in the United States by
Cherrytree Books
1980 Lookout Drive
North Mankato, MN 56001

U.S. publication copyright © Cherrytree Books 2005
International copyright reserved in all countries. No part
of this book may be reproduced in any form without
written permission from the publisher.

Library of Congress Cataloging-in-Publication Data
applied for

First Edition
9 8 7 6 5 4 3 2 1

First published in 2004 by
Evans Brothers Limited
2A Portman Mansions
Chiltern Street
London W1U 6NR
Copyright © Evans Brothers Limited 2004

Conceived and produced by

White-Thomson Publishing Ltd.

Consultants: Jean Mead, Senior Lecturer in Religious
Education, School of Education, University of
Hertfordshire; Dr Anne Punter, Partnership Tutor,
School of Education, University of Hertfordshire.
Designer: Carole Binding

Acknowledgments:
Special thanks to the following for their help and
involvement in the preparation of this book: Saadia
Durani, Dr. M. Ally Soodin, the people at the Jamia
Mosque, Watford, staff and children from Peartree
Spring Junior School, Stevenage.

Picture Acknowledgments:
Corbis: pages 15 top (Dean Conger), 18 left (Suhaib
Salem/Reuters).
All other photographs by Chris Fairclough.

Contents

What Is a Mosque?

A **mosque** is a special building where **Muslims** go to **pray**. Many mosques have a **dome**, and a tower called a **minaret**.

mosque   **Muslims**   **pray**

There are five times every day when Muslims pray. Muslims can pray at home, at work, or wherever they are, but many men go to the mosque to pray together.

▲ Which words describe the inside of this mosque? Is it

dark ✳ light ✳ clean ✳ colorful ✳ calm ✳ bare ✳ beautiful?

dome   minaret

Allah, the One God

Muslims pray to Allah. "Allah" is the Arabic word for God and in Arabic writing it looks like this.

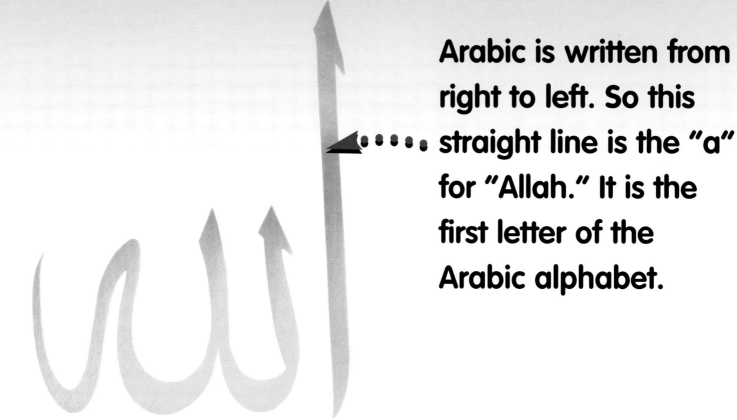

Arabic is written from right to left. So this straight line is the "a" for "Allah." It is the first letter of the Arabic alphabet.

Can you find where the name of Allah is written like this in the mosque on page 5?

Allah   Arabic   God

Muslims **believe** that Allah shows people the right things to do. They believe that Allah's words are written in their **holy book**, called the **Qur'an**.

▲ After school, Muslim children go to the mosque to learn to read the Qur'an.

believe   holy book   Qur'an   **7**

The Prophet Muhammad

Muslims believe that Allah sent messengers, to give people his words. The final messenger was the Prophet Muhammad. He lived in Arabia and spoke in Arabic.

▶ This is the Prophet Muhammad's name, in Arabic writing.

Whenever Muslims say or write his name, they add, "Peace be upon him." These words are written here.

Muslims believe that the Prophet Muhammad spoke words from Allah. They were written down to make the Qur'an.

▲ The Qur'an begins with "In the name of Allah." Can you see the word "Allah" on the first page of this Qur'an?

Arabia   peace

Writing and Patterns

▶ The mosque is decorated with Arabic writing and with patterns. Can you see the word "Allah"?

There are no pictures of Allah or the Prophet Muhammad in the mosque. Muslims think that people might worship the pictures instead of Allah.

decorated   worship

◀ The Arabic writing here says "There is no god but Allah and Muhammad is His messenger." The writing and patterns are made from colored tiles.

This alcove is called the mihrab. Everyone faces the mihrab to pray. You can find out why on page 18.

tiles   alcove   mihrab   11

A School Visit

▶ When people visit a mosque, they show respect by doing what Muslims do. They take off their shoes.

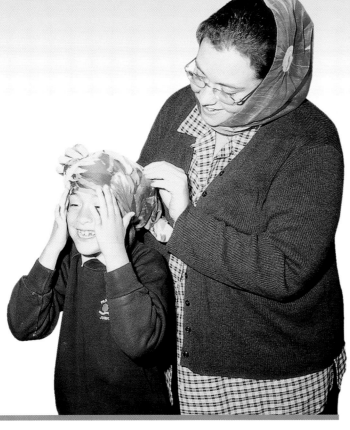

◀ Girls and women must wear a headscarf. Boys and men who visit the mosque do not need to cover their heads.

respect   headscarf   gallery

▼ Visiting a mosque can help you understand how Muslims pray. Muslim girls and women pray in this gallery. Muslim men and boys pray here.

cabinet for Qur'ans

prayer times board

mihrab

prayer beads

Which things in the mosque would you like to investigate?

prayer times   prayer beads   13

Times to Pray

A board in the mosque shows the five times of every day when Muslims must pray. The times change during the year, as the times of sunrise and sunset change.

1 Before sunrise

2 After midday

3 Mid-afternoon

▶ The second prayer time on a Friday is special, so it has its own clock on the board.

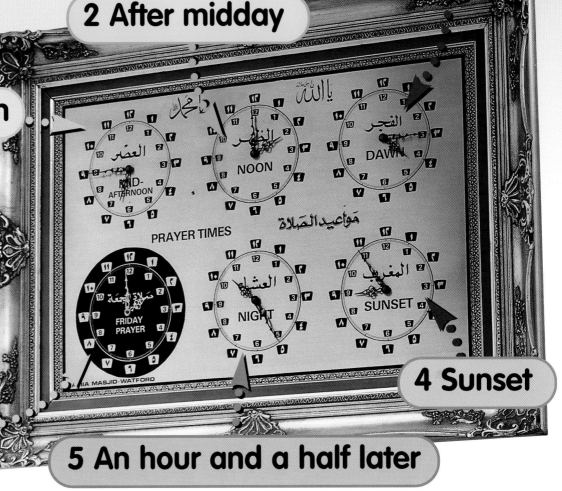

4 Sunset

5 An hour and a half later

The special prayer time on Fridays is called jumma prayer.
It is a time when many Muslims go to their mosque and mosques are full of people.

◄ Before jumma prayer, the imam gives a talk about Muslim life.
The imam is the man who leads the prayers in the mosque.

jumma   imam

Preparing to Pray

▶ Before each prayer time, a man called a muezzin calls out, in Arabic, that it is time to pray. This call to prayer is called the adhan.

◀ When people did not have clocks or watches, muezzins called the adhan from minarets. This still happens in some countries, but not usually in the United States.

16

muezzin   adhan

▼ Before they pray, Muslims wash in a special way called wudu. They wash hands, mouth, nose, face, arms, head, ears, neck, and feet three times each.

Many Muslim men and boys and all Muslim women and girls wear something on their head to pray.

wudu

Prayer Positions

All over the world, when Muslims pray, they face toward a building called the Ka'aba. It stands in the Grand Mosque in Makkah, in Saudi Arabia.

► In all mosques the mihrab shows the direction of the Ka'aba. So everyone faces the mihrab to pray.

▼ Muslims stand on a prayer mat to pray, and repeat this set of movements called a rak'ah.

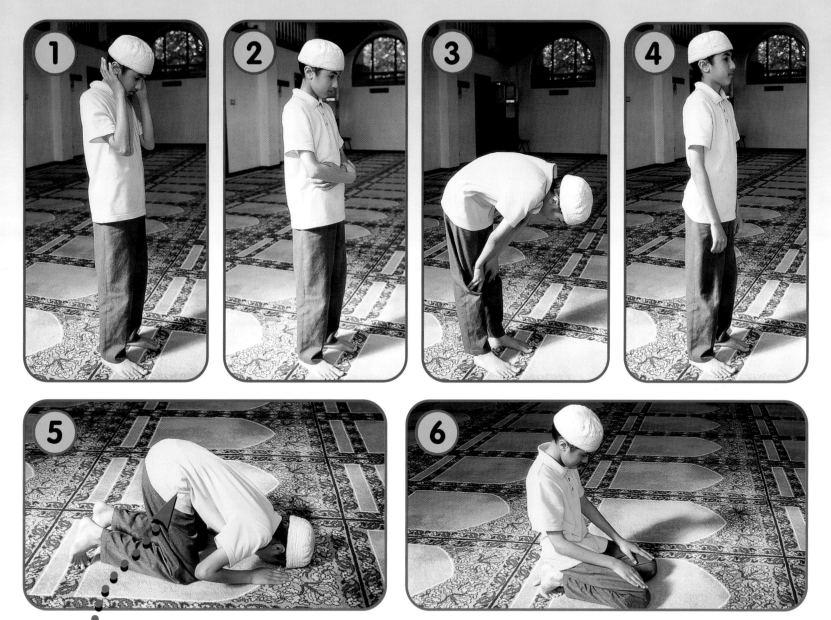

Bowing down is a way to say "I will do as Allah wants."

prayer mat   rak'ah

Learning Some More

Looking at special things in the mosque helps you learn about the Muslim religion, called Islam.

► You will see copies of the Qur'an, and the stands that Muslims use when they read it.

◄ You may see prayer beads that Muslims sometimes count as they say their prayers.

Islam

▶ You can also learn by talking to Muslims you meet at the mosque.

◀ Rajwan is showing how copies of the Qur'an are sometimes wrapped in cloth to protect them.

Look back at the Muslims you have seen in the mosque in this book. What questions would you like to ask them?

Further Information for

New words introduced in the text:

adhan	dome	jumma	muezzin	Prophet	worship
alcove	gallery	Ka'aba	Muslims	Muhammad	wudu
Allah	God	Makkah	peace	Qur'an	
Arabia	headscarf	messengers	pray	rak'ah	
Arabic	holy book	mihrab	prayer beads	respect	
believe	imam	minaret	prayer mat	Saudi Arabia	
decorated	Islam	mosque	prayer times	tiles	

Background Information

Pages 4-5: Mosque is the English word for *Masjid*, a Muslim place of worship. Traditionally this incorporates a dome, originally designed for good acoustics and air circulation, and a minaret for the call to prayer. Some mosques in the United States have been adapted from other buildings and so may not have these features. Mosques also serve as community centers. The prayer hall is used for the five daily prayers. Muslims arriving to pray stand shoulder to shoulder in rows, starting from the center front. It is forbidden for women to pray in front of men, as it is considered immodest and distracting, and so a separate gallery or room is usually provided. Prayers may be performed anywhere, on a clean place or prayer mat.

Pages 6-7: Muslims believe the Qur'an to contain the actual words of Allah, revealed to the Prophet Muhammad by the Angel Gabriel in Arabic. The Qur'an is always learned in that language. The Qur'an is treated with respect and not normally put on the floor or on laps. The Qur'an and Arabic books and cards open the opposite way to books in English. The after-school class is called a madrasah.

Pages 8-9: The Prophet Muhammad is regarded as the last of the prophets. He is never worshipped or thought divine, and it is inappropriate to call Muslims "Mohammedans". Everything known about the Prophet Muhammad is called the *Sunnah*, and Muslims use this as a source of guidance about life and practice. Collections of reports of the words and actions of the Prophet, known as the *Hadith*, are a part of the *Sunnah*. In English writing, Muslims use the abbreviation "p.b.u.h." (peace be upon him) after the Prophet Muhammad's name. Muslims also respect other biblical prophets, including Jesus (*Isa*) and Moses (*Musa*).

Pages 10-11: Above the *mihrab* is the *Shahadah*, the basic Muslim statement of faith. When leading prayers the *imam* faces into the *mihrab*. The "steps" in the photograph on page 11 are a pulpit for the Friday sermon (see page 15).

Pages 12-13: When preparing for a visit observe the appropriate etiquette. As shoes will be removed, ask children to have clean socks. Females should have a headscarf, and women should wear loose, modest clothing. In the mosque, avoid sitting with feet pointing toward the *mihrab*.

Parents and Teachers

Pages 14-15: The prayers said five times daily are called *salat*. They last about five minutes and are followed by personal prayer called *dua*. The prayers may be performed "in arrears" if it has not been possible to do them in the right time-slot. Friday is not a "day of rest," but Muslim men are required to pray in congregation for the Friday "after-midday" prayers if possible. (The top photo on page 15 shows Friday prayers at the Sultan Mosque, Singapore.)

Pages 16-17: The "d" in the words *adhan* and *wudu* is sometimes pronounced as if it is combined with a "z."

Pages 18-19: The *Ka'aba* is the focus of the *Hajj* pilgrimage, which commemorates the story of Ibrahim. The direction for prayer can be found using a special *qiblah* compass.

Pages 20-21: The Qur'an is usually kept on the highest shelf and placed on a stand to read. It is only handled after *wudu*. The prayer beads are called *tasbih* and are often used for personal prayers before or after the *salat*. There are usually 99 beads, divided into three sets of 33 for reciting "Glory be to Allah," "Thanks be to Allah," and "Allah is great."

Suggested Activities

■ Show pictures of a range of mosque buildings, and discuss what makes them mosques (use/design?).

■ Visit a local mosque or use a virtual visit.

■ Make thank-you cards after a visit, by sticking on gold-colored dome and minaret shapes.

■ Read some stories about the Prophet Muhammad, and other prophets mentioned in the Qur'an.

■ Make some calligraphy of the name of Allah by tracing or doing rubbings from plaques. How many times can children recognize the word in this book, or on a mosque visit? Let children make and decorate "calligraphy" of their own names, using cutout letters or two pencils tied together. Discuss the importance of names.

■ Make mosaic patterns.

■ Listen to the call to prayer, prayers, or verses from the Qur'an being recited in Arabic (tape, video or on a visit).

■ Talk about the value of preparing for something very special.

■ Look at and find out about some Muslim artifacts, treating them with appropriate respect.

■ Ask a Muslim child or visitor to tell about what *salat* and the mosque mean to him, or use a video clip.

Recommended Resources

BOOKS

Ghazi, Suhaib Hamid, and Rayyan, Omar. *Ramadan*. New York: Holiday House, 1996.

Knight, Khadijah. *My Muslim Faith* (Big Book). London: Evans, 1999.

Juma, Siddiqa. *Stories of the Prophets* (6 board books). Elmhurst, NY: Tahrike Tarsile Qur'an, Inc., 1999.

WEB SITES

The following sites provide an interesting introduction to Islam and Muslim worship generally.

http://home.sprynet.com~aalsabbagh
www.arabesq.com/Sabur/omy
www.islamcity.org/KidsCorner

Index